ST. THOMAS AND THE
WORLD STATE

Aquinas Lecture 1949

ST. THOMAS AND
THE WORLD STATE

Under the Auspices of the Aristotelian Society
of Marquette University

BY

ROBERT M. HUTCHINS

Chancellor,
The University of Chicago

MARQUETTE UNIVERSITY PRESS
MILWAUKEE
1949

To

MORTIMER ADLER

for twenty-two years

PREFATORY

The Aristotelian Society of Marquette University each year invites a scholar to deliver a lecture in honor of St. Thomas Aquinas. Customarily delivered on the Sunday nearest March 7th, the feast day of the Society's patron saint, these lectures are called the Aquinas Lectures.

In 1949 the Society had the pleasure of recording the lecture of Robert Maynard Hutchins, Chancellor of the University of Chicago.

Born in Brooklyn, N. Y. in 1899, Chancellor Hutchins attended Oberlin College 1915-17, served in the U. S. Army 1917-19, and received from Yale University his A.B. in 1921, an honorary M.A. in 1922 and LL.B. in 1925. He was master of English and history at Lake Placid School, 1921-23; lecturer in the Yale University law school, 1923-25; secretary of the University 1923-27; professor of Law 1927-29 and dean of the Yale University law school 1928-29. In 1929 he was appointed president of the University of Chicago and in 1945 became Chancellor.

He has been awarded the honorary degree of Doctor of Laws by West Virginia University, Lafayette College, Oberlin College (1929), Williams College (1930), Berea College (1931), Harvard University (1936), Tulane University (1938), the University of Copenhagen (1946), the University of Frankfurt (1948) and the University of Stockholm (1949); the University of Illinois gave him an honorary Doctor of Letters degree in 1947.

He holds the Italian Croce di Guerra and is an officer of the French Legion of Honor.

Chancellor Hutchins was chairman of the Commission of Inquiry on Freedom of the Press in 1946 and of the Committee to Frame a World Constitution in 1948.

He has made innumerable public addresses and contributed to many scholarly and popular periodicals.

He has published three books: *No Friendly Voice* (1936); *The Higher Learning in America* (1936), and *Education for Freedom* (1948).

To these the Aristotelian Society takes pleasure in adding *St. Thomas and the World State*.

ST. THOMAS AND THE
WORLD STATE

"*It is therefore to be hoped that the doctrines of Aquinas, concerning the ruling of peoples and the laws which establish their relations with one another, may be better known, since they contain the true foundations of that which is termed the 'League of Nations'*" (Pius XI *Studiorum Ducem*, 29 June 1923).

"*As formerly, when the Church contributed, after the mediaeval fashion, to the political moulding of Europe, it seems that today she is aware of her duty to contribute, after the fashion of our modern age, and thanks to the moral authority which is everywhere recognized as being hers, to the salvation of our threatened civilization, to the social shaping of the world and the advent of a new order*" (Maritain *Ransoming the Time*, p. 204).

St. Thomas and the World State

IN THIS lecture I propose to show how St. Thomas, beginning with the remark of Aristotle that the state is the perfect community, transmuted that remark into a political theory relevant in every age; and how this theory, together with the teachings of St. Thomas in the *Treatise on Law,* leads irresistibly in our day to world law, world government, and a world state.

I

Aristotle said in the *Politics,* "But, if all communities aim at some good, the state or political community, which is the highest of all, and which embraces all the rest, aims, and in a greater degree than any other, at the highest good."[1]

He went on: "But when several families are united, and the association aims at something more than daily needs, then comes into existence the village. . . . When several villages are united in a single community, perfect and large enough to be nearly or quite self-sufficing, the state comes into existence originating in the bare needs of life, and continuing in existence for the sake of a good life. . . . Besides, the final cause and end of a thing is the best, and to be self-sufficing is the end and the best. . . . The proof that the state is a creation of nature and prior to the individual is that the individual, when isolated, is not self-sufficing."[2]

These observations must be taken, as their author implies, as the statement of an ideal. Herodotus and Thucydides do not portray the Greek city-state as aiming at the highest good; certainly they do not portray it as achieving it. And when Aristotle wrote, the city-state had long passed its prime. Nor can it be said the city-states had been in any sense self-sufficing. The aggrandizement of Athens must have borne some relation to the fact that Athenians did not feel self-sufficient, either with respect to defense or with respect to material goods, within their own borders. Even the conservative Spartans had not confined their hegemony to their own walls.

Aristotle was concerned to show the origin of the state and the aims of the state. In doing so he laid down the attainment of autarky or self-sufficiency as a measure of what he conceived the state to be.

These hints, for they are nothing more than that, St. Thomas took to build a political theory comprehensive, coherent, and flexible. In the *Treatise on Law* he used the language of Aristotle to define the aims of political organization. He said, "As one man is a part of the household, so a household is a part of the state: and the state is a perfect community, according to *Politics I, 1.* And therefore as the good of one man is not the last end, but is ordained to the common good; so too the good of one household is ordained to the good of a single state, which is a perfect community."[3]

In *De Regimine Principum* he went beyond Aristotle and the city-state. He said, "Now since men must live in a group, because they are not sufficient unto themselves to procure the necessities of life were they to remain solitary, it follows that a society will be the more perfect the more it is sufficient unto itself to procure the necessities of life."[4]

Up to this point St. Thomas is merely paraphrasing Aristotle. But he goes on: "There is, indeed, to some extent sufficiency for life in one family or one household, namely in so far as pertains to the natural acts of nourishment and the begetting of offspring and other things of this kind; it exists, furthermore, in one village with regard to those things which belong to one trade; but it exists in a city, which is a perfect community with regard to all the necessities of life; but still more in a province because of the need of fighting together and of mutual help against enemies. So, the man who rules a perfect community, that is, a city or a province, is called a king *par excellence.* . . ."[5]

By this time it had become clear that a city might not be a perfect community; without the aid of the surrounding territory it might not be able to protect itself. The meaning of "state" had changed since Aristotle's day, because the state that might have been self-sufficing in his day was now far from it.

In *De Regimine Principum* St. Thomas tells us flatly what it means to be self-sufficing. He says, "For the higher a thing is the more self-sufficient it is; since whatever needs another's help is by that fact proven inferior."[6] We must look, then, for a political organization that does not need another's help if we are to discover the perfect community.

In the *Commentary on St. Matthew* St. Thomas looks beyond the province. His words are: "The community is threefold: that of the household, of the city, and of the kingdom. The household is a community consisting of those through whom common acts are done; it consists of a triple union, of father and son, of husband and wife, of master and servant. The community of the city contains all things that are necessary to the life of man: therefore it is the perfect community as far as those things that are merely necessary. The third community is that of the kingdom, which is the consummate community. For when there is fear of enemies, it is not possible for a city to subsist by itself; hence on account of fear of enemies it is necessary for there to be a community of many cities, which make one kingdom."[7]

It would appear that, however perfect the household may be for certain purposes, and the city for other purposes, there are still other, and more inclusive, purposes that neither can fulfil. The most important of these is peace, which Aristotle, curiously enough, nowhere seems to regard as one of the essential conditions of the perfect community. In the *Commentary on St. Matthew,* St. Thomas continues: "As life is in a man, so is peace in a kingdom; and as there can be no health without moderation of the humors, so there is peace when a body retains its proper order. And as when health declines, the man verges toward his death, so when peace declines, the kingdom verges toward its death. So that the ultimate thing that must be sought is peace."[8]

This note of peace as characteristic of the perfect community is struck also in *De Regimine Principum,* where St. Thomas says, "Now the welfare and safety of a multitude formed into a society is the preservation of its unity, which is called peace, and which when taken away, the benefit of social life is lost and moreover the multitude in its disagreement becomes a burden to itself."[9]

Later on in the same work the same point is elaborated. St. Thomas says, "Yet the unity of man is brought about by nature, while the unity of a society, which we call peace, must be procured through the efforts of the ruler. Therefore, to establish virtuous living in a multitude three things are necessary. First of all, that the multitude be established in the unity of peace. Second, that the multitude thus united in the bond of peace be guided to good deeds. For just as a man can do nothing well unless unity within his members be presupposed, so a multitude of men which lacks the unity of peace, is hindered from virtuous action, by the fact that it fights against its very existence as a group. In the third place, it is necessary that there be at hand a sufficient supply of the things required for proper living, procured by the ruler's efforts."[10]

St. Thomas then mentions some hindrances to the conservation of the state and adds, "The third hindrance to the preservation of the state comes from without, namely when peace is destroyed through the attacks of enemies, or, as it sometimes happens, the kingdom or city is completely blotted out."[11]

According to St. Thomas, then, the perfect community is one that does not need the help of another, that is at peace, and that can by its own will and resources remain so. Any other community must be an accidental or inadequate organization of power. It cannot be "self-sufficing."

Nor does the mind of St. Thomas fail to notice the community of the whole world, to which St. Augustine had referred in *The City of God.* St. Augustine's words were: "After the city follows the whole world, wherein the third kind of human society is resident, the first being in the house, and the second in the city. . . ."[12] To Augustine also the aim of the earthly community is peace; for he goes on to say, "And the heavenly city, or rather that part thereof which is as yet a pilgrim on earth and lives by faith, uses this peace also, as it should until it leaves this mortal life wherein such a peace is requisite . . . it willingly obeys such laws of the temporal city as order the things pertaining to the sustenance of this mortal life, to the end that both cities might observe a peace in such things as are pertinent hereunto. . . . This celestial society while it is here on earth, increases itself out of all languages, being unconcerned by the different temporal laws that are made; yet not breaking, but observing their diversity in divers nations, so long as they tend unto the preservation of earthly peace, and do not oppose the adoration of one God alone. . . . This peace is that unto which the pilgrim in faith refers

the other peace, which he has here in his
pilgrimage; and then lives he according to
faith, when all that he does for the obtaining
hereof is by himself referred unto God, and
his neighbour withal, because being a citizen,
he must not be all for himself, but sociable
in his life and actions."[13]

He goes on: "Wretched then are they that
are strangers to that God, and yet have those a
kind of allowable peace, but that they shall
not have for ever, because they used it not well
when they had it. But that they should have
it in this life is for our good also; because
during our commixture with Babylon, we ourselves make use of her peace, and though faith
does free the people of God at length out of
her, yet in the meantime we live as pilgrims
in her. And therefore the apostle admonished
the Church to pray for the kings and potentates
of that earthly city, adding this reason, 'that
we may lead a quiet life in all godliness and
charity.' And the prophet Jeremiah, foretelling
the captivity of God's ancient people, com-
manding them (from the Lord) to go peace-

ably and patiently to Babylon, advised them also to pray, saying, 'For in her peace shall be your peace,' meaning that temporal peace which is common both to good and bad."[14]

This recognition of a world community by St. Augustine, in his intense concern for peace, has a parallel in St. Thomas. The exigencies of peace brought him to regard the kingdom, a larger political entity than the city, as a more perfect community than the city. In his *Commentary on the Sentences,* St. Thomas goes on to the whole world. He says, ". . . and between a single bishop and the Pope there are other grades of dignities corresponding to the grades of unions insofar as *one congregation or community includes another one,* as the community of a province includes the community of the city, and the community of the kingdom includes the community of the province, and the community of the whole world includes the community of a kingdom."[15]

II

St. Thomas does not deal with the possible political organization of the community of the whole world. But we know from the *Treatise on Law* that any political community requires human law, why it requires it, and what that law is. We know that divine law and natural law are not enough; positive law must be added. This law, in order to prove an efficacious inducement to virtue, must have coercive power.[16] And sometimes, at least, this law must be written, in order to supply what was wanting to the natural law; or because the natural law was perverted in the hearts of some men, as to certain matters, so that they esteemed those things good which are naturally evil.

St. Thomas sums up the matter thus: *"On the contrary, Isidore says: Laws were made that in fear thereof human audacity might be held in check, that innocence might be safeguarded in the midst of wickedness, and that the dread of punishment might prevent the wicked from doing harm.* But these things are most necessary to mankind. Therefore it was necessary that human laws should be made. . . . But since some are found to be depraved, and prone to vice, and not easily amenable to words, it was necessary for such to be restrained from evil by force and fear, in order that, at least, they might desist from evil-doing, and leave others in peace, and that they themselves, by being habituated in this way, might be brought to do willingly what hitherto they did from fear, and thus become virtuous. Now this kind of training, which compels through fear of punishment, is the discipline of laws."[17]

The positive law, according to St. Thomas, applies with coercive power to everybody but the sovereign. He says, "The sovereign is said to be *exempt from the law*, as to its coercive power; since, properly speaking, no man is coerced by himself, and law has no coercive power save from the authority of the sovereign. . . . But as to the directive force of law, the sovereign is subject to the law by his own will. . . . Again the sovereign is above the law, in so far as, when it is expedient, he can change the law, and rule within it according to time and place."[18]

We see, then, that in the hands of St. Thomas the Aristotelian conception of the perfect community underwent an important transformation. St. Thomas did not feel bound to limit himself to the state of Aristotle; he saw that the city might often fail to provide those things which were merely necessary; and he saw that peace was the most necessary thing of all. He was prepared to adopt an evolutionary attitude toward the state and to recognize that changing conditions might make thoroughly unsatisfactory a form of political organization that was once adequate to men's needs. What was a perfect community at one stage of history might be highly imperfect at another stage. He was not unprepared to regard the whole world as a community.

Because of the fallen state of human nature divine law and natural law are not enough to produce the unity of peace. Political organization requires positive law. The political organization of the world community would require positive law on a world scale. It would require legislative, judicial, and executive organs to adopt, declare, and enforce the positive law of the world. This law would be necessary to regulate and control the sovereigns of extant states, who are exempt from the operation of the positive law of their states and who cannot be regulated and controlled by divine and natural law alone. These extant states, in the absence of positive law of the world, may be expected to act toward one another as individuals may be expected to act in the absence of positive law; they may be expected to break the peace.

III

If we follow the example of St. Thomas and ask ourselves what is the perfect community today, we see by the light he has given us that not even on the economic level can any extant state be regarded as self-sufficing in the Thomistic or even the Aristotelian view of it. There is no state that does not need the help of another. As Father DeRooy has pointed out, particular states are specialized, each in a certain way.[19] No one of them has at its disposal all material resources and all the varieties of material goods that men can today reasonably want and use. The industrial changes that have taken place since the time of Aristotle mean that even as to those things which are merely necessary the extant states are not self-sufficing.

When we come to that which St. Thomas thought the real sign of self-sufficiency, namely, peace, we see again that there is no state that does not need the help of another. We observe, too, that the divine law and the natural law alone will not suffice to save us from destruction. War is inevitable among sovereigns who are not controlled by positive law, each of whom wants what the other has, who are close together, and who are equipped with military force. In the world as it is today all sovereigns want what other sovereigns possess, and modern transportation has brought them all close together, and will bring them closer still. The United States and Russia are as close together as Athens and Sparta were in the fifth century before Christ.

The military force available to modern sovereigns exceeds anything of which Aristotle and St. Thomas could have dreamed. The difference is one of kind; we now have weapons against which there is no defense. Peace cannot be preserved by defenses when there is no defense. Peace cannot be preserved by overwhelming force when a small supply of atomic bombs can inflict irreparable damage on both sides; no force will look overwhelming to a sovereign that has an adequate supply of these bombs. As war is inevitable in a world of sovereigns uncontrolled by positive law, so the destruction of civilization is inevitable if war breaks out after more than one nation has atomic bombs. Since we know that it is merely a matter of a few years until more than one nation has atomic bombs, we may say that unless sovereigns can be controlled by positive law it is merely a matter of a few years until civilization is destroyed.

Arnold Toynbee has said, "About the year 1875, it looked as though Europe would find equilibrium through being organized into a number of industrialized democratic national states. . . . We can now see that this expectation of equilibrium, on the basis of the national unit, was illusory. Industrialism and democracy are elemental forces. . . . What we can now pronounce with certainty is that the European national state . . . is far too small and frail a vessel to contain these forces. The new wines of industrialism and democracy have been poured into old bottles and they have burst the old bottles beyond repair."[20]

Fortunately, new bottles are available to us if we have the courage to use them; for the same forces that have made the destruction of civilization inevitable in the absence of positive law enforceable against nations have prepared for us a world that can be united by law, since it is already one world. Upon this point Toynbee insists over and over again. He says, "The main strand of our modern Western history is not the parish-pump politics of our Western society as inscribed on triumphal arches in a half-dozen parochial capitals or recorded in the national and municipal archives

of ephemeral 'Great Powers.' The main strand
is not even the expansion of the West over the
world — so long as we persist in thinking of
that expansion as a private enterprise of the
Western society's own. The main strand is the
progressive erection, by Western hands, of a
scaffolding within which all the once separate
societies have built themselves into one. From
the beginning, mankind has been partitioned;
in our day we have at last become united[21]
. . . as far as we know for certain, the only
civilization that has ever become world wide
is ours. . . .[22] As a result of these successive
expansions of particular civilizations, the whole
habitable world has now been unified into a
single great society. . . .[23] The historians of
A.D. 4047 will say that the impact of the
Western civilization on its contemporaries, in
the second half of the second millennium of
the Christian era, was the epoch-making event
of that age because it was the first step towards
the unification of mankind into one single
society. By their time, the unity of mankind
will perhaps have come to seem one of the

fundamental conditions of human life — just part of the order of nature — and it may need quite an effort of imagination on their part to recall the parochial outlook of the pioneers of civilization during the first six thousand years or so of its existence. Those Athenians, whose capital city was no more than a day's walk from the farthest frontiers of their country, and those American contemporaries — or virtual contemporaries — of theirs, whose country you could fly across from sea to sea in sixteen hours — how could they behave (as we know they did behave) as if their own little country were the universe? . . .[24]In the course of its expansion our modern Western secular civilization has become literally world-wide and has drawn into its net all other surviving civilizations as well as primitive societies."[25]

In this capture of the world by western civilization Toynbee sees a great new opportunity for Christianity. His words are: "At its first appearance, Christianity was provided by the Graeco-Roman civilization with a universal state, in the shape of the Roman empire with its policed roads and shipping routes, as an aid to the spread of the Christianity around the shores of the Mediterranean. Our modern Western secular civilization in its turn may serve its historical purpose by providing Christianity with a completely world-wide repetition of the Roman Empire to spread over."[26]

IV

In view of this opportunity, in view of the historical vision of the Church as the Church Universal, in view of the dreadful consequences of another war, and in view of the teaching of St. Thomas, it is not surprising that Popes and Bishops and other Catholic thinkers should have insisted upon the unity of the world.

Benedict XV, in 1920, said, "It would be truly desirable . . . that all states should put aside mutual suspicion and unite in one sole society or rather family of peoples. . . ."[27]

Pius XI said in 1922, "We forget that all men are our brothers and members of the same great human family."[28]

Pius XII has many times discussed the government of this great human family. In his first allocution, in 1939, he called for an international juridical institution, and warned the nations to bear in mind the experience gained from the ineffectiveness or imperfections of previous institutions of the kind.

In his Christmas allocution a few months ago the Pope attacked "the aberrations of an intransigent nationalism which denies or spurns the common bonds linking the separate nations together and imposing on each one of them many and varied duties toward the great family of nations."[29]

"The Catholic doctrine on the state and civil society," the Pope said, "has always been based on the principle that, in keeping with the will of God, the nations form a community with a common aim and common duties."[30]

He pointed out that, "Even when the proclamation of this principle and its practical consequences gave rise to violent reactions, the Church denied her assent to the erroneous concept of an absolutely autonomous sovereignty devoid of all social obligations."[31]

As to the support that Catholics should give
to movements for world organization, he said,
"The Catholic Christian, persuaded that every
man is his neighbor and that every nation is a
member, with equal rights, of the family of
nations, cooperates wholeheartedly in those
generous efforts whose beginnings might be
meager and frequently encounter strong opposition and obstacles, but which aim at saving
individual states from the narrowness of a self-
centered mentality."[32]

The American Bishops, in November, 1944,
demanded that positive international law govern relations in the international community.
This law was to be universal in scope. Positive
international law must be interpreted by a
world court, the decisions of which should
be judicial, not advisory; and these decisions
should be enforced.[33]

So Father DeRooy has said, "Nature has
given us the general lines of the organization
of States. This work must be continued and
made clearer by the work of men. . . . A com-
plete positive organization of international so-

ciety would demand the following institutions:
1) A human authority well defined under the
authority of God. 2) A legislative power to
make precise and to develop the precepts of
natural law and to put them in contact with
contingent and changing reality. 3) An executive power with an international coercive force
to assure the application of the laws and the
judicial decisions. 4) A judicial power to judge
all international litigations which have not
been resolved by other peaceful means such
as arbitration."[34]

Father Hensler has expressed the same
views. He says, "It (the League of Nations)
was ineffective principally because it lacked
genuine coercive power against recalcitrant nations. . . . The Pope does not consider it
enough to urge nations to observe the natural
moral law in their dealings with another. The
natural law itself cannot be an ideal code; it
must be supplemented and reinforced by positive law. . . . Not only have the nations of
the world the obligation of organizing the international community, but the duty of sub-

mitting to its authority in all that pertains to
the common good of all mankind. . . . The
freedom of nations in their dealings with one
another is exactly akin to the freedom of individuals. It consists not in the right to be a
law unto themselves, but to live under a higher
law. The right concept of national independence, therefore, is freedom limited by law as
determined and enforced by the appropriate
authority of the international community. . . .
The international juridical institution which
the Pope desires to be established will have
the task of determining the extent to which
nations may act as free agents in the international sphere."[35]

Don Sturzo, in his attack on war, has noticed that history changes the rights and duties
of states, as St. Thomas noticed that the ex-
panding needs of cities, and their increasing
dangers, changed the conception of the perfect community. He says, "To the objection
that the wars of the ancient Hebrews were
legitimate and that 'God willed' the Crusades,
it must be answered that Moses authorized

family vengeance (*Numbers* iii), that poly-
gamy was accepted by Abraham, that slavery
was in use among the ancient Hebrews. If
the abolition of such practices has done no
violence to Holy Scriptures, the same may be
said of the abolition of war."[36]

Don Sturzo then goes on to tell us what
world government means. His words are: "In
an organized international community an ag-
gressor state must be defined as one that either
has recourse to arms or prepares for a war,
even to vindicate a right which was unjustly
violated. In such a community, no State will
have any more right to take up arms of its own
accord than a private citizen in a national community to take the law into his own hands and,
without recourse to a tribunal of justice, to
vindicate his own right or demand reparation
for an injury or restitution for damage that has
been done him. . . . The fundamental impera-
tive of the common good imposes new limitations on the Heads of national Governments;
and one of these limitations is the inability to
vindicate national rights by any other means

than recourse to the established juridicopolitical system which has taken from individual States the initiative in war."[37]

Don Sturzo insists upon the point that historical change has changed the conception of the perfect community, a point upon which St. Thomas had insisted before him. Don Sturzo says, "The root of the matter is that there exists in nature and according to nature an international community, and that such a community, however potentially, imperfectly and tentatively, has always existed, even though at times it has been clothed in the dress of hegemonic power (as in the case of the Roman Empire) or of theocratic authority (as in the case of the Holy Roman Empire or Christendom or of the Padisha for the Mohammedans, or of the Empires of the Sons of Heavens or of the Sun for the Chinese or Japanese). If there have been in the past several centers of international unification rather than a single one, that was a consequence of two simple facts: first, the lack of geographic unification — the human race did not know itself fully because communications between the various continents were few and difficult; second, religious differences at a time when common allegiance depended largely on unity of belief, and when Christians themselves could be divided as they were into Eastern and Western Churches.

"But now that modern ways of thinking have widened the separation between political and religious life while, at the same time, intercontinental communication has become more frequent, less difficult, and, in the air, extremely rapid, the possibility of ecumenical unification has become more and more a reality. Today, under pressure of the tragic events of two world wars, it is becoming a *fait accompli.*"[38]

V

But here arises an apparent contradiction, which has confused some Catholics and seems destined to confuse more. Whereas Popes, Bishops, and Catholic thinkers seem to favor world government, they also seem to favor the independence of sovereign states, and sometimes to regard divine and natural law as enough for the government of that community which they unanimously discern in the world.

Thus in 1939 Pius XII called for an international organization "which, respecting the rights of God, will be able to assure the reciprocal independence of nations big and small."[39] Later in the same year he said, "A fundamental postulate of any just and honorable peace is an assurance for all nations, great or small, powerful or weak, of their right to life and independence."[40]

So the American bishops, after calling for what looks like a world government, say, "The international organization must never violate the rightful sovereignty of nations. Sovereignty is a right which comes from the juridical personality of a nation and which the international organization must safeguard and defend."[41]

Such language seems to have bewildered Father DeRooy, who, as we have seen, demands a world executive, a world legislature, a world court; in short, a world government. He says, "The family is a society intrinsically incapable of attaining its end if it is not in a State, whereas the State is a perfect society in the sense that it has by itself all the means necessary for attaining its end. It is not a question of attaining its end through international society; it can attain that end by itself. . . . We must take care then not to transpose simply to the state in respect of international society the relations of subordination which hold between the individual and the family as parts in respect of the state as a whole. This subordination is nowhere near so great."[42]

In spite of his demand for positive international law, Father DeRooy says, "But how does free will intervene to realize it (the common good of international society) in the concrete? Simply in observing the natural law which rules the common life of the states."[43] Again he says, "Thus in the last instance the international life of States is measured by the Eternal Law, and proximately by the natural law."[44]

Father DeRooy goes on, in asserting the right of the State to sovereign independence:

"This right is founded on the fact that the State as a perfect society possesses an end and the means for realizing that end independent of any other civil society. Consequently, its authority does not depend on any authority superior to it (independence) and it must be sovereign to establish the means for attaining its end. This sovereignty is both interior and exterior. . . . Exterior sovereignty is manifested in the right of active and passive legislation, the right of negotiation and the right to make war and peace. The limits of sovereignty are fixed by the natural and divine law, by the right of the international community and by positive pacts and customs."[45]

This position, if it is to be literally interpreted, is sufficiently demolished by Don Sturzo, who, as we have seen, demands a juridico-political system that takes from individual States the initiative in war. He says, "Such a limitation, it is sometimes argued, is incompatible with national sovereignty. The argument is based on the premise that the State is a perfect society (to use the language of

Scholasticism) that can accept none but the self-imposed limitations from which it may, and sometimes must, withdraw according to the dictates of its own best interests; and this, without any violation of natural or Christian ethics.

"The error that vitiates the argument is the assumption that the State is the only natural and necessary society; as though the same were not true of the international community, merely because it is supposed to be a purely voluntary society. It must be remembered — what is too often forgotten by those who make this assumption — that there have been periods in the history of our civilization when there were no States (in the modern sense of the word), and that the cities which were the centers of political power were later unified into larger territories by kings or princes who ruled over federations or dynastic kingdoms with little in common beyond the bond of allegiance to the same lord. If one but recalls the patriarchal period, or the periods of family and tribal rule, it becomes obvious that the so-called 'political' power can exist, actually or virtually, in other social groups than the modern State. Or if one thinks of the vast empires in the past which have included many subject but separate kingdoms (or even of modern instances) it should be clear that political power has been vested in various manners and with varying degrees of responsibility."[46]

Don Sturzo states his cardinal position thus: "The concept of the State as a 'perfect Society' is not absolute; it is relative to the functions of a society which is supposed to be able, by its own means, to achieve a specific end. But when a particular society is no longer able to attain this specific end, except in collaboration with other societies of the same kind, it becomes a duty to collaborate. And, consequently, there arises a mutual interdependence, and rights and duties are shifted to the new community. This is the case of the individual who can no longer, by himself, achieve his end. It is the same with families, with cities, with nations, with modern States. The society resulting from collaboration realizes the purposes of individual members, but at the same time, transcends them in the name of the common good."[47]

VI

The contradiction in the views of popes, bishops, and Catholic thinkers is, I believe, more apparent than real. I think these dignitaries and philosophers mean what Don Sturzo means, though I must add that it would be useful if they would say so in such a way that there could be no possibility of mistaking them. I think they know that the national state is no longer the perfect community and that positive law is required to make the world community an effective political organization. I believe that they are making two points that are of the utmost importance: first, they are saying that any world government must be a federal government; and second, they are saying that world government must come into existence by consent and not by conquest.

When the American bishops say that the state has a natural right to sovereignty, they do not intend to display any fondness for the

modern state in its nationalistic manifestations.
The main line of Catholic thought about the
modern national state reflects a desire to re-
duce rather than to enlarge its growing power.
The principle of subsidiary function in *Qua-
dragesimo Anno* and the pluralism of Maritain
both show this desire.[48] Nor can this saying
arise in Catholic thought from any opposition
to world government. This saying originated
long before anybody was seriously for or
against world government.

When we say that a state has a natural
right to sovereignty, we mean that a people
has the natural right to rule itself. A people
is a group of human beings, sufficiently numerous and sufficiently prepared by experience
and diversity of talent to constitute a state,
that is, a perfect society. Its perfection lies in
its supposed adequacy with respect to the end
of human association — the common good. The
fact that a community is perfect does not mean
that it is perfectly closed. It does mean that
it is entitled to enter freely into relationships
with other communities of a similar kind, and

that it cannot rightfully be forced into such relationships.

The origin and meaning of the saying that a state has the natural right to sovereignty, therefore, is that one state may not forcibly impose its will upon another. It means that Catholics should oppose the foundation of a world state by force. It cannot mean that Catholics should oppose the formation of a world state by consent. If it did, it would mean that the natural rights of thirteen sovereign states were violated at the birth of the American Republic. This saying guarantees existing states the natural right to decide for themselves whether they will join a larger union. The naturalness of the right to self-rule is not contradicted when a given state freely decides to give up its supremacy; the naturalness of the right is preserved in the freedom with which it gives it up.

From many quarters, East and West, we now hear the demand for world government by conquest. Against this demand the Catholic doctrine of a natural right to self-rule will be a great protection. By the same sign Catholic doctrine should be a strong argument for world government by consent, and all Catholics should, it would seem, be ardently working for it.

VII

Let me summarize the history of the doctrine. Throughout the age of nations there is at least one persistent strain in Catholic thought. From the Catholic tradition of jurisprudence there came the most effective denials of the absolute sovereignty of nations. Catholic jurists, as Catholics, were not bound to any one of the nation-states, nor to any form that any one of them took. By no means indifferent to developments in the earthly city, but from the secure vantage-point of a primary interest in the city of God, Catholic jurists were strong proponents of the existence of an international society. The assertion of the existence of an international society and the denial of absolute sovereignty to nations were equivalent statements.

A society exists only where there is a common end somehow commonly pursued. The common good or end for this international society, the existence of which Catholic tradition steadily asserted, could only be the good human temporal life that all human beings, equal in nature, naturally desire.

The nations that composed this international society were not absolute sovereigns. There was only one Absolute Sovereign. For the natural life of man God had made one decree promulgated by His creative word, the word that created human nature. Natural law, conceived as a participation of eternal law, is that decree. Natural law is but a preceptive expression of the Divine intention for man's temporal existence as that intention is contained in the natural inclinations of men for the perfection possible to men as men.

But Catholicism with its immense experience in the law, Roman and canon, and with that greatest of all books on the philosophy of law, St. Thomas's *Treatise on Law,* to guide it, could not be naive about the inadequacy of natural law to maintain order in the world. The end of human society, though fixed and measured by natural law, requires for its existence and direction determinations of natural law, in the form of human law delivered by authorities given the power to enforce its directive intent. If experience is needed to support the point that any society will be inadequately directed by natural law alone, the experience of international society in the age of nations can be readily called to mind. Pacts and leagues have fallen short of what the Thomistic definition of positive law requires.

The Catholic tradition, then, points clearly toward the necessity of world government. In the measure that Catholics have had better grounds than have those whose life was more completely immersed in earthly nations for denying sovereignty to nations and for asserting the existence of an international society, and in the measure that Catholics have had St. Thomas's incomparably lucid analysis of positive law for the establishment, maintenance, and progress of any society, Catholics have, then, always been virtually for world government. They have always known that the society of nations can never be maintained in order and peace without the institution of positive law, giving determination, authority, and coercive power to the rule of natural law.

The existence of a world society, of a family of nations, which popes and Catholic jurists have always asserted, implies, then, world law and world government. The only perfect community today is a world state. It is the only community that is self-sufficing. Every smaller community requires, in the phrase of St. Thomas, the help of another.

VIII

What is indicated, therefore, is a clear call for world government on the part of the Church and active leadership in the movement for world government on the part of its members. Certainly in advance of such a call and such leadership it cannot be assumed that no world government can meet Catholic claims. Catholics cannot work for a world state radically hostile to the Church, no matter what

alleviation of temporal distress that state might
bring to suffering people; for Catholics cannot
support a state that does violence to aspirations
transcending the human temporal condition.
Catholics cannot work for a world state that
would suppress freedom of religious worship,
teaching, and communication. But Catholics
can make plain the kind of world state that
they can work for. If it then appears that such
a world state is impossible, Catholics will at
least have shown mankind once more the road
it ought to have taken. Surely it is too early
to say that mankind would not take that road
if the Church and its members pointed the way.

In any world state that could be organized
in our time Europe, the West, and Christendom
would be out-numbered. Yet it does not seem
that the West should lack confidence that all
that was good in its civilization would find a
proper estimate in a world that was kept in
order. It appears probable that the West would
rediscover the elements of that goodness in
itself. Nor does it seem consonant with the

missionary tradition of the Church to feel over-whelmed by the numbers of the unfaithful.

Catholics have much to deplore in the shrinkage of Europe, the spread of atheistic communism, the cold war of great powers, the inflamed state of those diseases, Class and War, which have killed all the civilizations that have died, the threat of losing in a world-wide catastrophe the great contributions that western civilization and western Christendom have made. Catholics, though they are prepared in the assurance of everlasting life for the Church to begin in any small corner untouched by ex-plosion, cannot wish universal destruction nor feel content with the tremendous tensions that exist while there is fear of its possibility. Catholics must be eager that Europe and the West should not only survive, but also revive and reacquire a deeper conception of human civilization than the one recently current, which centers around a religion of progress by re-sourceful greed and technological mastery of non-human nature. It is doubtful that there is a better way by which the West can revive

secularly than by dedicating its remaining initiative to the cause of world government, a
world government that would be just to all
men, that would embody the best thoughts,
experience, and institutions of the western tradition and provide for the awakening East
room for political and spiritual growth. No
Catholic would argue that the many lost sheep
in the East are not sheep of the same Shepherd
or that the only way to get them back into the
fold is to slaughter them or their leaders.

Yet we know that world government is
coming by conquest or consent. As Catholics
do not want to be conquered by the Russians,
so they should not want to conquer them.
Since it is equally repulsive to conquer and to
be conquered, Catholics might consider the
conditions under which, as citizens of countries
throughout the world, they and their countries
should consent to a world government. The
motion toward world government is that motion in our time which carries with most purity
an appeal to the aspirations of men for peace
and justice. It is the best means by which the

divinely sanctioned institutions of law and government can be used to improve the temporal lot of mankind. According to the mind of St. Thomas, only the world state can now be the perfect community.

St. Thomas said that peace was the work of charity and justice, of charity directly and of justice indirectly.[49] The work of religion and the church is charity. The work of the state and government is justice. Church and State — universal church and world state — must now work together for world peace founded on universal charity, which would realize the brotherhood of man, and universal democracy, which would bring justice to all mankind.

NOTES

1. *Op. cit.*, I, 1, 1252a3-6.

2. *Ibid.*, I, 2, 1252b14-1253a27. Cf. II, 2, 1261b13: "A city only comes into being when the community is large enough to be self-sufficing."

3. *Summa Theologica*, I-II, q. 90, a. 3, ad 3.

4. *De Regimine Principum*, Book I, Ch. 1.

5. *Ibid*.

6. *Ibid.*, Book II, Ch. 3.

7. *In Evangelia S. Matthaei Commentaria*, Ch. xii. I am indebted to my friend William Gorman for this text. There appears to be a distinction in this passage between a perfect community and a community of consummation or a consummate community. The city is said to be perfect with regard to those things which are merely necessary for the life of man. But it is also said that the city cannot subsist by itself in peace, and for this reason St. Thomas argues that "it is necessary for there to be a community of many cities, which make one kingdom." Now if peace is necessary for the life of man as well as for the existence of the political community itself, then the community which cannot by itself secure peace for itself and its citizens can hardly be called perfect even with regard to those things which are merely necessary. The word "consummate" signifies something in excess of "perfect" only if peace is a luxury rather than a necessity—only if the life of man and the city can

be well-lived without peace, however advantageous peace may be as an added condition.

8. *Ibid*. Aristotle does not say that "the ultimate thing that must be sought is peace." On the contrary, he says that the legislator must keep neighboring countries in mind "because the state for which he legislates is to have a political and not an isolated life. For a state must have such a military force as will be serviceable against her neighbors and not merely useful at home. Even if the life of action is not admitted to be the best, either for individuals or states, still a city should be formidable to enemies, whether invading or retreating" (*Politics*, II, 6, 1265a20-27). The political life of the individual may be a life of peace under the laws of the state, but the political life of the state is a life of war which Aristotle admits is not the best life for the state any more than it would be the best sort of life for the individual.

9.   *Op. cit.*, Book I, Ch. 2.

10.   *Ibid.*, Book I, Ch. 15.

11.   *Ibid.*

12.   *City of God*, Book XIX, Ch. 7.

13.   *Ibid.*, Ch. 17. Cf. Book XII, Ch. 21, in which St. Augustine says: "Though he was not left solitary, for there is nothing so social by nature, so unsocial by its corruption as this race of man, yet one individual man was created first. And human nature has nothing more appropriate either for the prevention of discord, or for the healing of it

where it exists, than the remembrance of the first
parent of us all, whom God was pleased to create
alone, that *all men* might be derived from one,
and might thus be admonished to *preserve unity*
among their *whole multitude.*"

14. *Ibid.*, Book XIX, Ch. 26.

15. *Op. cit.*, IV, d. xxiv, q. III, a. 2, gla. 3. I am
indebted to Father DeRooy for this text which he
quotes in Lecture X of the *CIP Course in Politics.*
The possibility of a world-wide political community seems to suggest itself to St. Augustine
and St. Thomas by comparison with the world-
wide religious community of the universal church.
It may be thought that the fact that St. Thomas
goes beyond Aristotle in proposing the kingdom
as a larger and more inclusive community than the
city, and "the community of the whole world" as
the most inclusive society, is to be explained by
the difference between the political perspectives
of the 4th century B. C. and the 13th century A. D.
But such an explanation would leave a certain text
in Aristotle unexplained.

In *Politics*, VII, 4, Aristotle says: "To the size
of states there is a limit, as there is to other things,
plants, animals, implements; for none of these
retain their natural power when they are too large
or too small, but they either wholly lose their
nature or are spoiled" (1326a35-40). The state,
he goes on to say, "when composed of too few is
not, as the state ought to be, self-sufficing; when
of too many, though self-sufficing in all mere
necessaries, as a nation may be, it is not a state,

being almost incapable of constitutional government" (1326b1-5). And the reason he gives at this point is failure in communication.

To this there are two answers: one is the institution of representative government as that is developed only in the modern world; the other is the power of the technical means of transport and communication now available. As Aristotle could not conceive the possibility of "a ship a quarter of a mile long," so he could not conceive the possibility of a state the size of the United States in 1789.

But Aristotle offers another reason for thinking that the size of the state must be severely limited in territory and population. "Law is order," he writes, "and good law is good order; but a very great multitude cannot be orderly: to introduce order into the unlimited is the work of a divine power" (*ibid.*, 1326a29-32). To this there are also two answers. First, the world community is not "unlimited" in size, even though it is the largest possible community on earth. Second, the comparison of historic communities, large and small, does not support the statement that "a very great multitude cannot be orderly" or the implication that the government of a small community will be better government than the government of a large community. Aristotle admits that the limit in size must be "ascertained by experience" (*ibid.*, 1326b 12) ; and he thinks that "experience shows that a very populous city can rarely, if ever, be well governed; since all cities which have a reputation for good government have a limit of population" (*ibid.*, 1326a24-27). The appeal to experience leaves Aristotle with too little experience to defend his position.

Aristotle himself says certain things which suggest a contrary line of reasoning. He criticizes those who "judge of the size of the city by the number of the inhabitants; whereas they ought to regard, not their number, but their power" (*ibid.*, 1326a10-11). "A city, like an individual," he says, "has a work to do; and that city which is best adapted to the fulfillment of its work is to be deemed greatest" (*ibid.*, 1326a11-12). But if the work the state has to do includes the preservation of peace, it may be argued that the larger community can succeed where the smaller community must fail.

Furthermore, Aristotle considers the size and wealth of a city in relation to the inevitability of war. "A city," he writes, "which produces numerous artisans and comparatively few soldiers cannot be great" (*ibid.*, 1326a23). In another place, criticizing the proposals of Phaleas, he says that "the government must be organized with a view to military strength; and of this he has not said a word. And so with respect to property; there should not only be enough to supply the internal wants of the state, but also to meet dangers coming from without. The property of the state should not be so large that more powerful neighbors may be tempted by it, while the owners are unable to repel invaders; nor yet so small that the state is unable to maintain a war even against states of equal power. . . . A more powerful neighbor

must have no inducement to go to war with you
by reason of your wealth, but only such as he
would have had if you had possessed less"
(*Politics*, II, 7, 1267a20-31).

Cf. *ibid.*, III, 9, 1280b30-1281a1 where Aristotle makes consanguinity a condition of the good
city; and *ibid.*, VII, 5, where he discusses the extent of territory required in order that the citizens
may "live at once temperately and liberally in the
enjoyment of leisure."

16.   *Summa Theologica*, I-II, q. 90, a. 3, ad 2.

17.   *Ibid.*, I-II, q. 95, a. 1.

18.   *Ibid.*, I-II, q. 96, a. 5, ad 3. What St. Thomas
here says about the sovereign prince applies without the slightest alteration to the sovereign state.

19.   Vd. the *CIP Course in Politics*, New York, Catholic International Press, 1945, Lecture X, pp. 4-5.

20.   *Civilization on Trial*, New York, 1948, p. 114.

21.   *Ibid.*, p. 91.

22.   *Ibid.*, p. 101.

23.   *Ibid.*, p. 158.

24.   *Ibid.*, pp. 215-216.

25.   *Ibid.*, p. 238.

26.   *Ibid.*, p. 239.

27.   Encyclical, *Pacem Dei*.

28. Encyclical, *Ubi Arcano*.

29. Christmas Allocution, 1948.

30. *Ibid.*

31. *Ibid.*

32. *Ibid.*

33. Reported in full in the *New York Times*, November 19, 1944, p. 40. "International law," the Bishops declared, "must govern international relations. Might must be subordinate to law."

34. *Op. cit.*, Lecture X, p. 6.

35. In a paper delivered at a conference of the clergy of the Diocese of Pittsburgh, printed in the *Pittsburgh Catholic*, Sept. 30, Oct. 7, Oct. 30, 1944; and reprinted in the *Catholic Mind*, Nov. 1944, pp. 692-700.

36. "The Influence of Social Facts on Ethical Conceptions" in *Thought*, Vol. XX, No. 76, March, 1945, p. 123, note 4.

37. *Ibid.*, p. 105.

38. *Ibid.*, pp. 106-107.

39. Response to the Homage of the New Minister of Haiti, Nicolas Leger (reprinted in *Principles of Peace*, Washington, 1943, p. 622).

40. Christmas Allocution (reprinted in *Principles of Peace*, pp. 632-640; the passage cited is in paragraph 1497).

41. *Loc. cit.* in fn. 33 *supra.*

42. *Op. cit.*, Lecture X, p. 5.

43. *Ibid.*

44. *Op. cit.*, Lecture XII, p. 8.

45. *Ibid.*

46. *Op. cit.*, pp. 105-106.

47. *Ibid.*, p. 106, note 5.

48. Vd. Maritain, *True Humanism*, New York,
1938, Ch. 3-5. Cf. Yves Simon, *Nature and Functions of Authority*, Milwaukee, 1940, esp. pp. 46-
47, where Professor Simon formulates the cor-
relative principles of authority and autonomy. The
Principle of Authority is stated as follows:
"Wherever the welfare of a community requires
a common aciton, the unity of that common action
must be assured by the higher organs of that community." The Principle of Autonomy is stated as
follows: "Wherever a task can be satisfactorily
achieved by the initiative of the individual or that
of small social units, the fulfillment of that task
must be left to the initiative of the individual or
to that of the small social units." These two principles should guide us in determining the authority
to be granted to the political organs of world
government, and in determining the autonomy to
be retained by the various levels of local government and economic administration down to the
smallest units.

49. *Summa Theologica,* II-II, q. 29, a. 3, ad 3:
"Peace is the *work of justice* indirectly, in so far
as justice removes the obstacles to peace; but it is
the work of charity directly, since charity, according to its very nature, causes peace."

THE AQUINAS LECTURES

Published by the Marquette University Press,
Milwaukee 3, Wisconsin

∽∾∿

St. Thomas and the Life of Learning (1937) by the
late Fr. John F. McCormick, S.J., professor of
philosophy at Loyola University.

St. Thomas and the Gentiles (1938) by Mortimer J.
Adler, Ph.D., associate professor of the philosophy of law, University of Chicago.

St. Thomas and the Greeks (1939) by Anton C.
Pegis, Ph.D., president of the Pontifical Institute
of Mediaeval Studies, Toronto.

The Nature and Functions of Authority (1940) by
Yves Simon, Ph.D., professor of philosophy of
social thought, University of Chicago.

St. Thomas and Analogy. (1941) by Fr. Gerald B.
Phelan, Ph.D., director of the Mediaeval Institute, University of Notre Dame.

St. Thomas and the Problem of Evil (1942) by
Jacques Maritain, Ph.D., professor of philosophy,
Princeton University.

Humanism and Theology (1943) by Werner Jaeger,
Ph.D., Litt.D., "university" professor, Harvard
University.

The Nature and Origins of Scientism (1944) by Fr. John Wellmuth, S.J., Chairman of the Department of Philosophy, Xavier University.

Cicero in the Courtroom of St. Thomas Aquinas (1945) by the late E. K. Rand, Ph.D., Litt.D., LL.D., Pope Professor of Latin, *emeritus*, Harvard University.

St. Thomas and Epistemology (1946) by Fr. Louis-Marie Régis, O.P., Th.L., Ph.D., director of the Albert the Great Institute of Mediaeval Studies, University of Montreal.

St. Thomas and the Greek Moralists (1947, Spring) by Vernon J. Bourke, Ph.D., professor of philosophy, St. Louis University, St. Louis, Missouri.

History of Philosophy and Philosophical Education (1947, Fall) by Étienne Gilson of the Académie française, director of studies and professor of the history of mediaeval philosophy, Pontifical Institute of Mediaeval Studies, Toronto.

The Natural Desire for God (1948) by Fr. William R. O'Connor, S.T.L., Ph.D., professor of dogmatic theology, St. Joseph's Seminary, Dunwoodie, N. Y.

St. Thomas and The World State (1949) by Robert M. Hutchins, Chancellor of The University of Chicago.

⚬~⚬

First in Series (1937) $1.00; all others $1.50
Uniform format, cover and binding.